PATIOS AND GARDENS OF MEXICO

by PATRICIA W. O'GORMAN

Photographs by Bob Schalkwijk

ARCHITECTURAL BOOK PUBLISHING COMPANY

New York 10016

Library of Congress Cataloging in Publication Data
O'Gorman, Patricia.
    Patios and gardens of Mexico.
    1. Patios—Mexico. 2. Gardens—Mexico.   I. Schalkwijk, Bob.
II. Title.
NA8375.036   728'.9   79-17263
ISBN 0-8038-0210-2

Published simultaneously in Canada by
Saunders of Toronto, Ltd., Don Mills, Ontario.

Printed in the United States of America

To Mr. and Mrs. Warren Shipway,
to whom we owe so much inspiration,
this book is dedicated.

CONTENTS

Delightful Don Cresencio Ramirez is the very heart and secret of the beautifully kept Restaurant San Angel Inn gardens. All the gardens and patios you will see here are tended by *jardineros* of many different skills and still more varied and romantic names; there are Gumercindos, Pantaleones, Faustinos and even Salomes. To quote the great Mexican poet, Carlos Pellicer, "Two things distinguish the Mexican above all, his taste for color and his love of flowers." These humble men are truly in love with what becomes, in their earth-stained hands, an art.

One of Helen O'Gorman's enchanting sketches of the clock vine, which is called *cielo azul* in Mexico because of its blue flowers. This vine does extremely well in gardens in Cuernavaca.

To the many who have enjoyed and been inspired by the Shipways' books on the architecture, artifacts and gardens of Mexico, the continuation of this series by Patricia Von Waberer O'Gorman and the talented photographer, Bob Schalkwijk, will be welcome as a source of ideas and materials so abundant in Mexico.

Mexico is a never ending reservoir of architectural design due to its topographical conditions and its climate, which is conducive to pleasing outdoor living, but even more because of its double heritage, of the fabulous pre-Hispanic gardens and palaces and of the importations of the Spanish, which already had been enriched by the exotic strains they had acquired from the Greek, Roman and Islamic cultures in the form of Persian ceramics, carved fountains and doorways and beautiful courtyards. The natural ingenuity and craftsmanship already in this country in the New World were and still are the means of continuing a unique and rich expression in building and decoration.

Patricia Von Waberer O'Gorman is particularly qualified to present this collection of material—having grown up amid the richness of Mexico's traditions and having put the best of these to modern use artistically as she has done in her building of homes in San Miguel de Allende.

Helen F. O'Gorman

ACKNOWLEDGMENTS

We wish to thank very specially Mrs. Nina Lincoln for her constant and indispensable advice and support, and Mr. Javier Tinoco for his indefatigable efforts in the photographic laboratory.

Also, Mrs. Katherine Walch, Mr. and Mrs. John Beadle, Mrs. Helen O'Gorman who so kindly lent us her beautiful flower drawings, Mrs. Sloane Simpson, Mr. Robert Brady and Mr. Peter Bubela, without whose help, talent and encouragement this book would never have been produced.

In addition, our warmest thanks to the many kind people who allowed us to photograph their houses and gardens and made it such a delightful experience.

AUTHOR'S NOTE: As a matter of clarification, the term *convento* is used to denote both monastery or convent. Furthermore, since all religious buildings in Mexico are government property they are referred to as "former *convento*" in this book.

PICTURE LOCATIONS

PATIOS AND GARDENS OF MEXICO

Home of Josue and Jaqueline Saenz

The truly magnificent house built by Mr. and Mrs. Josue Saenz opens into this rather austere but brilliantly sunny patio which can be seen through the simple iron gate. The center arch in the background is topped by a delicately wrought iron ornament.

Opposite page: Inside the patio of the former *Convento* of Cuitzeo in the state of Michoacan, one can savor and become immersed in what is truly, in all its elegance, massiveness and sobriety, the Colonial Architecture of the sixteenth century.

This *Convento* of the Augustinian Order was built at the same time as the *Convento* of Yuriria nearby. From these *conventos*, missionaries departed to make converts in distant places. These converts in turn were put to work to build more treasures of Colonial Architecture.

The severity of these great arched stone walls is relieved and lightened by the formally laid out planting in the patio, as usual surrounding a stone well head.

Former Convento of Cuitzeo, Michoacán

In great contrast to the classical order of the preceding page, this stunning house makes ample use of a new architectural style which takes its inspiration from many different sources. This style, in fact, is becoming much the fashion of building in today's Mexico. In spite of combining many different architectural features, it achieves a sense of unity. Mr. Possenbacher, a well-known collector, has furnished and decorated the house with many of his beautiful objects.

These two photographs show the entrance patio from different angles. The paving is made of specially rounded brick set into 1½″ borders of white cement. The interesting balustrade is fashioned out of terra cotta forms put in sideways. As in many houses in Cuernavaca, the windows are barred with carved wooden railings.

Home of Michael and Nicolette Possenbacher

Museo Ex-Convento de San Gabriel de Barrera

This beautiful old Hacienda was built by the Count of Valenciana in 1770, but during the course of the years has undergone many transformations, some fortunate, others not. At the beginning of this century, the owner tried to impose on it a Frenchified atmosphere greatly at odds with its colonial simplicity. However, he did much to keep up the gardens and didn't attempt to remodel the main house, which is now extremely well restored and maintained by the State of Guanajuato. A set for many films and a place for official receptions, this lovely former Hacienda was visited by the Queen of England and President Kennedy when they came to Mexico.

The patio is the traditional double-arched eighteenth century structure. The carved stone arches are supported by square columns, and a simple iron railing guards the upper corridor.

3

Home of Helen Ford

The entrance to this house, built by Rodolfo Ayala in Cuernavaca, shows a very imaginative use of water. The little fountain is the center of the eight-sided star on the pavement, which is made of fragments of stone and glazed tile. To one coming in from the blinding hot sun, this Moorish-inspired court gives a cool and pleasant introduction to the rest of the house.

San Angel

The tranquil and elegant old district of San Angel is one of the most sought after places to live in the City of Mexico. Tradition and a convent-like peace rise up from its very cobblestones and its high bougainvillea-covered walls. Here, and in neighboring Coyoacán, are to be found the most beautiful patios, gardens and houses to which we were given privileged access. The residents of San Angel are as resistant to change now as they have been for centuries. Madame Calderon de la Barca, in her delightful book, *Life in Mexico*, notes that the Indians of this charming village refused to "permit the innovation of restoring the roads and streets."

5

Plaza of the Archangels is the charming name Arquitecto Alejandro von Wuthenau has given his beautifully designed little public square in San Angel. In its center is a large old carved stone fountain. At each corner are placed large semi-circular masonry benches with the name of each of the archangels carved in stone above them. Shade and coolness are provided by tall trees covered with cascading vibrantly colored bougainvillea.

By far the most amusing garden inscription is carved on a slightly crooked and broken obelisk. "Mas vale la gracia de la imperfeccion, que la perfeccion sin gracia." (The grace of imperfection is more to be valued than perfection without grace.) Happily, in this case the little square is perfection with grace.

Plaza de los Arcángeles, Mexico City

Among great gardens in Mexico City, one of the most exceptional and interesting is the garden and patio of Mr. and Mrs. Larrea's elegant home. Facing the large French doors of the dining room is a beautifully designed Italian inspired formal water garden. Surrounding an old palm tree, four equi-distant and identical shallow pools are set into an intricate floor mosaic. Seen through the fine mist produced by the water jets, the soft pinks, greys and golds of the floor mosaic make it seem a veritable magic carpet.

This sculpture of a boy on a dolphin has the dolphin spouting water into a little side fountain, adding to the Italian flavor of the water garden. Facing west is the Colonial patio, which has access to the imposing entrance to the house. Four symmetrical flower beds planted with rose bushes and orange trees surround a very simple octagonal stone fountain. Much valued for their wonderful perfume, orange trees are a traditional feature of colonial patios.

Home of Jorge and Sara Larrea

Patios have been put to multiple and interesting uses, but none more so than the loftily arched patio of an old colonial house in San Angel. This has been converted into a delightful craft center, restaurant, and *the* place to spend one's Saturdays in the City. The central fountain is piled high with skillfully arranged flowers or fresh fruit. Around this are set tables for an *al fresco* meal while a marimba band plays. In the surrounding arcades, little booths display varied crafts in metal, ceramics, yarn, paper, and even sugar.

Bazar Sábado

10

Originally the Hacienda de Goicochea, it has been restored and made into one of the most elegantly traditional restaurants in Mexico City. Built in the early eighteenth century, this hacienda was the home of the Spanish Count of Pinillas and later of the Adalid family, who turned its 90,000 acres into producing pulque, the native cactus drink. In the huge rectangular main patio, one can sit under the covered arcades and admire the skillful planting of the low flower beds around the oval central fountain. Ever flowering bougainvillea covers the high walls and adds much color to this lovely courtyard.

One of the many decorative details to be found in the Restaurant San Angel Inn is this candlestick of wrought iron and glass.

11

Home of Sloane Simpson

In complete contrast with the traditional atmosphere of the previous pages, Mrs. Sloane Simpson's light and airy patio in Acapulco commands a beautiful view of the sea. The house takes its name, Villa del Arbol, from the huge light yellow-trunked amate tree, which gives shade to the patio.

Below: The Club de Vela de la Peña in Valle de Bravo was built by Arquitecto Andres Casillas, who knew how to assimilate and blend into his design the many natural resources of this lovely lakeside village. Again, this master of the new architectural style prevalent in Mexico astonishes with the force of simplicity, where frivolity or over-decoration would be sacrilege. His exteriors also, like this small patio, show that understatement which is so effective.

Club de Vela de la Peña, Valle de Bravo

Posada Carmina, San Miguel de Allende

If one looks for a perfect example of a provincial colonial patio, the one at Posada Carmina in San Miguel de Allende would be a very good choice.

This detail from the same patio shows an interesting feature. It has a second-story stone reservoir which helped to avoid the necessity of fetching water from downstairs from the main fountain.

Built on the slopes of the Popocatepetl volcano in the early sixteenth century over the main spring that supplied the village of Ocuituco with water, this convent is now abandoned and in a sad state of disrepair. The four lions, covered with lichen, still look down into the main fountain. They have recently been copied and placed on a fountain at the entrance to Cuernavaca.

Former Convento of Ocuituco

Unknown Patio

Perhaps this photograph can convey the feeling of interior peace that is the main attraction of a convent patio. Although in a sad state of decay, it retains the evidence of better days.

The Villa, as it is fondly thought of by one and all in San Miguel de Allende, is another example of the many uses given to the domestic patio. This house originally belonged to Fray Jose Mojica, well known in San Miguel as a famous opera singer. He left fame, family and house to become a Franciscan monk. The present owner, much loved Mrs. Betty Kempe, shares with the good friar a passion for remodelling, and has done much to improve it. Most of the rooms of her house (formerly a hotel) open into this patio, centered around the inevitable fountain. The covered arcades around the patio were furnished for the indoor/outdoor enjoyment of the guests who gathered around the lovely carved stone fireplace in the evenings. The massive columns supporting the wide arches are made of masonry. The tiled, sloping roofs are most uncharacteristic in this part of Mexico.

This is Arturo, who makes the most awful noise at the worst possible times (especially at the siesta hour), but gives a beautiful and colorful touch.

16

The recent restoration of the beautiful old Hacienda of Galindo owes its great elegance to the taste of Xavier Barbosa. This architectural designer of great merit knows how to translate the feeling of the old into the comfort of the new without losing the original spirit of dignity in the process. The enormous central grass-covered patio is flanked on two sides by traditionally covered arcades, where masonry arches are supported by simple stone columns. The two remaining sides give access to a convention center and to the swimming pool area. According to an old legend, the first mention of this hacienda says that Hernán Cortez, the conqueror of Mexico, built it to give as a gift to his interpreter and great love, La Malinche. What we do know is that it was built in 1546 and that it was in its time one of the richest and most extensive haciendas in Mexico. Since its restoration it has become a luxurious and exclusive hotel.

Hotel La Mansión Galindo

An interesting way to round off stone steps to include the corner.

17

Centro Cultural El Nigromante, San Miguel de Allende

An attractive use for large buildings with grand patios is to convert them into centers for cultural activities. In San Miguel de Allende, the government art school is housed in this former convent, built in the eighteenth century by the order of Sisters of the Immaculate Conception.

Surrounding the magnificent patio on all sides are high-ceilinged arched corridors that dwarf the human scale. Above all, there is an atmosphere of peace and quiet, occasionally enriched by the sound of music made by students practicing.

Opposite page: On a less grand scale, but of great cultural importance to San Miguel de Allende, is the Public Library. This achievement of Mexican-American understanding centers around the charming sunny patio. Tall, bushy cypresses are planted in front of the massive square stone pillars that support the arches. Color is provided by geraniums in pots around the fountain. The ground is paved with a combination of large, square stones making a pattern with small pebbles. White cotton umbrellas cover small tables where bookworms gather to read in the mornings and students chatter like magpies in the afternoons.

Biblioteca Publica de San Miguel de Allende

Former Convento of Coatlinchán

A WORD ABOUT PATIOS—THE WHYS AND WHEREFORES

It can be truthfully said that the patio is the heart of all Spanish colonial architecture. Whether domestic, religious or civil, no building of importance during this time was constructed without one or several patios. A passion for privacy and Spanish antipathy to the sun (in those days a pale complexion was considered desirable) are the two main reasons for the existence of the patio. A fountain or wellhead is always to be found in the center. The space surrounding this focal point was made into a formal garden usually planted with roses or other sweet smelling flowers as well as orange and lime trees. The high walls and arcades that enclosed the patio were covered with flowering vines, which added color and warmth to their austerity. Vegetables and fruit trees were relegated to the back orchard and never allowed to disgrace the patio.

To suit their different purposes, people in today's Mexico still look to the patio as a charming tradition to incorporate into their houses.

This primitive patio is interesting mainly because it is one of the earliest examples of colonial architecture. The heaviness of the stone workmanship makes one think that the native craftsmen had shortly before been engaged in building pyramids.

Opposite page:

The outdoor sitting space has been added to this attractive house in the course of its recent remodelling. It has greatly enlarged the living possibilities, since the owner is able to use this space for informal entertaining. The beamed ceiling is held up by a massive master beam, the exposed end of which has been carved into the traditional *pecho de paloma*. This, in turn, is supported by stone columns crowned by elaborate capitals. The wrought iron balustrade over the balcony is partly antique and partly made to match.

House in San Miguel de Allende

This tile-roofed loggia is both a refuge from the sun and an informal place to entertain by the poolside. The long benches and small table are built of masonry and form an integral part of the structure.

Opposite page:

It is difficult to imagine why these little tile-roofed shelters were built in the water. However, they probably appealed to the Emperor Maxmilian, who was said to have spent much time in these gardens during his famous *ocios* (getting away from it all). Here he was swung on a hammock by lovely female natives, which one feels must have contributed to the downfall of his empire. Built in the eighteenth century by the son of the silver king, Jose Borda, these now sadly neglected gardens still enjoy great popularity.

22

Drawing by John Beadle

Jardín Borda, Cuernavaca

This beautifully tile-roofed loggia at the edge of Mr. and Mrs. Possenbacher's pool in Cuernavaca gives shade to the swimmer, its contour follows exactly the shape of the pool and the pavement is made by interspacing stone squares with very small pebbles.

An extension of the dining room, this shelter, supported by two massive columns, provides added space for outdoor living. It is furnished with a harmonious combination of contemporary furniture and some excellent antiques from the owner's collection.

Home of Michael and Nicolette Possenbacher

A beamed overhang shades the luncheon table in Mr. Brady's charming garden. The chairs are made of iron but have the look of Viennese bent wood.

This cool and pleasant outdoor living room looks over the pool and through a stone balustrade into a semi-wild ravine overgrown with vines and many-colored bougainvillea. Against the stark white walls, the lime-green painted furniture and upholstery give a light and airy atmosphere.

Home of Robert Brady

Home of Allen and Jean-Claire Salsbury

25

Home of Rafael and Enriqueta Casasola

In a small area, the owners have been able to create very attractive outdoor-indoor living spaces.

Home of Alexander Kirkland

Undeniably, in Mexico, land of eternal sunshine, the sun is much venerated as a symbol of light and warmth. In the stone carving here the sun smiles happily on the exquisite Cuernavaca garden. Used as a cornerstone, it helps support the tiled roof.

Home of Milton and Sabina Leof

The indoor/outdoor feeling is captured to perfection in this enchanting dining room; the contrast between the sobriety of the dark-beamed ceiling, polished antique furniture and glowing colonial paintings on the one hand, and on the other the light and gaiety of the garden, make this room a total success.

This strange post-Columbian figure is half indigenous tiger and half Christian representation of the Lamb of God, strangely uniting these two cultural traditions.

Delightful *al fresco* meals are served in this loggia in a rambling, vine-covered Tepoztlán home.

Against the fantastic natural setting of Tepoztlán (a village near Cuernavaca surrounded by gigantic rock formations that at a distance look like fortified castles), this newly built adobe house is entered through the covered portico, which serves also as a small sitting area.

House in Tepoztlán

Home of Bob and Nina Schalkwijk

Romantically nestling below the massive Tepoztlán crags is the country hideout of Mr. and Mrs. Schalkwijk. Tile-roofed and rambling, it affords comfortable informality and accommodates their large brood and many friends. The combination of apricot and whitewashed walls is beautifully enhanced by climbing flame vines (*llamarada*) and arbors covered with russet bougainvillea.

Below: These two whimsical terra cotta flower pots show the imagination of native craftsmen from Acatlán in the State of Puebla, who sell them in the Tepoztlán market on Sundays.

Ruins of Labná

This extraordinary shelter-like structure forms part of the Mayan ruins of Labná in the State of Yucatán.

Below: Remote and primitive, the village of Pinotepa de Don Luis tells us much about its character through these simply tiled arcades, which have been the basic inspiration for many grander shelters. The columns that support the roofs are all masonry and almost all different.

Opposite page: Impressively constructed of palm leaves bound together by lianas, this palapa roof is the most natural, coolest and most elegant of shelters in tropical areas. This one in Cancún, seen from underneath, shows the readily available materials used in its construction and the skill of the native craftsmen.

Palapa in Cancún

Oaxaca, Village of Pinotepa de Don Luis

A veritable jewel, this understated example of the simple and sculptural form of architecture is the work of Arquitecto Marco Antonio Aldaco in Acapulco, for which he deserves special mention. The continuous fluidity of movement of these massive walls combined with the delicate and novel way he has found to roof the sheltered areas give this house a total sense of rightness. These sheltered areas are roofed by tying simple tree branches with cane, making a webbing to support the terra cotta tiles, and naturally bent tree trunks form the supporting columns. Also, his use of color, contrasting the almost blinding whitewashed interior walls and floors with the subtle, warm brownish pink color of the exteriors is masterly.

Casa Emilia, Acapulco

Drawing by John Beadle

Simply designed terra cotta pots are set in eye-catching places. The largest of these hold massive Areka Palms. These pots rest on heavy untreated wood bases under which small bowls catch the water or earth that seeps out and could stain the immaculate white surfaces.

The small garden is marvelously landscaped. From everywhere one gets a clear view of the deep blue ocean. Except for a border of pale blue plumbago, all the vegetation is green. The boundary of the property is marked by a huge planter filled with incredible fine-leaved ferns.

Palapa, Acapulco Beach

Just being finished as a bar on the beach in Acapulco is this interesting palapa. Most ingenious is the use of bamboo to give air from the top and to divide the area of the counter space. A low fence of palm tree trunks tied together with rope encircles the mellow brick floor laid on the sand.

Below: Casa de Mara is an outstanding example of what can be done to remodel a house with taste and imagination. The severe lines of this open living room are softened by the wicker furniture painted white and piled with off-white cushions. To this, lime green accessories add a touch of color. Facing the Bay of Acapulco, this sheltered space is cooled by the breeze and has a unique ambience of elegant simplicity.

Casa de Mara

Framed by the tall arch, the view into the sunny patio
with the sea as a background is strikingly beautiful.

Home of Sloane Simpson

Club de Golf Cancún

The course was laid out by famous golf course designer Robert Trent. The shelter is built in modern Maya style, covered by these interesting palapa roofs.

Below: The outdoor glory of Mexico are its magnificent beaches. A recent favorite is Cancún in the State of Quintana Roo. A little circle of sand plants grows around a copy of a well-known Mayan figure, Chac-Mool. The simple palapas make it all look most inviting.

Beach in Cancún

Whimsically old-fashioned is this cast iron gazebo found in an old garden in Mexico City. It was probably brought over from Europe during the Porfirian era when such things were much in vogue. It serves now to shelter musicians or caterers at big garden parties.

Home of Marcelo and Angela Javelly

This secretive and overgrown old corridor gives one the true feeling of enclosure that was a prerequisite of many of Coyoacán's oldest houses. The owners have had the sense and taste not to disturb this atmosphere.

Home of Maximilian and Elena Michel

Against a ancient ivy-covered wall stands this stone statue of a little girl, bringing a touch of delicate beauty to the austere old garden that faces it.

Home of Federico Patiño

Among the best architectural styles to be found in Mexico is one that, for want of a better name is called "Architecture of Demolition." Houses built in this manner are truly delightful mixtures of period, style and objects. When tastefully combined, as is the case in the home of Mr. and Mrs. Patino, the result can be surprisingly original. Entering from a small court into the main patio, one passes through an imposing square stone doorway. Nearby are arches from an old Puebla house.

A high column supports a little angel and fragments of beautifully carved stone from demolished houses are used to support flower pots. The square patio centers on a simple, large brick planter filled with ferns and pink azaleas. The walls surrounding it are roughly stuccoed and painted a light ochre. The ironwork is painted black, as is the cast iron trellis which supports the glass roof that makes this a novel kind of shelter. White wicker furniture gives it the finishing, nineteenth century, touch.

39

Museo ex-Haciendo San Gabriel de Barrera

The upper arcade of the Hacienda San Gabriel de Barrera is entered through a delicate carved wooden gate. Near it is a duplicate gate that closes off a niche where the water filter is kept. This beautifully formed niche is unique in that it is closed by a carved wooden gate on both sides, thus allowing light and air to come into the stairwell. This system of filtering water through a hollow, conical-shaped stone was used extensively in colonial households to purify drinking water, which also acquired a delicious, fresh flavor.

40

Home of Inez Havermale

This open, wide corridor is in constant use as an extension of the living room. Framed by massive stone arches, a long vista of the colorful garden delights the eye. A great gardener, the enchanting owner is constantly changing the color and hues of her annuals, so that every season brings a new surprise. In colonial times this house was a tannery and the owner has converted one of the tanks where the hides were soaked into a swimming pool, which is spanned by a graceful stone arch.

Below: A typical example of an open corridor in a colonial building is this charming looking one in the Hacienda de Cieneguilla.

Hacienda de Cieneguilla

Another covered area in the same style, in which the play of different heights demonstrates the use of simple, rough-cut wooden beams.

Valle de Bravo, most undeservedly, has not been given the recognition it merits. This charming old tile-roofed village overlooks a lovely lake surrounded by pine forests. Sailing enthusiasts have recently started to build very attractive weekend homes in the town and on the slopes of a nearby huge rock formation.

Home of Jesús and Yolanda Morales

View of Valle de Bravo

Home of José and Dolores Yturbe

Home of José and Dolores Yturbe

Designed by Arquitecto José Yturbe Bernal in the new style of architecture prevalent in Mexico today, this house possesses great simplicity and takes advantage of wood which, in Valle de Bravo, is plentiful. The open-air living room overlooks the lake and faces a little terrace surrounded by a low stone wall.

Guarding the entrance of his master's house as he once did in life, this carved stone dog is a loving memento.

Home of Xavier Barbosa

Imaginatively using this corner of the terrace wall, a bench of masonry follows its contours. The two little tables in the foreground are carved out of stone.

Below: In the grand manner, the Rancho San Joaquin in San Miguel de Allende turns back the clock to a more elegant way of life. With his unerring taste and eye for detail, the owner has, while preserving great airiness and light, given his house the true feeling of the almost extinct haciendas. From this vast, covered terrace one overlooks a formal garden and an avenue of orange trees which leads to a pond and continues to an open air amphitheater.

Home of Xavier Barbosa

45

San Angel, Mexico City

A beautiful stucco shell tops this finely carved antique door guarding the secrets of the garden behind it.

Opposite page: In the Hotel Las Hadas, these palms seem to rise majestically over the intricate mosaic pavement. The paths around the mosaic are made of square cut hard stone.

Las Hadas

Villa Alejandra, in Acapulco, combines a great variety of styles. Since it was first built, remodelling and redecoration have constantly altered it. Last to be built, a Moorish style pavilion is entered through this arch, partly shading the antique door that is a veritable gem of woodcarving. Depicting two saints in the upper panels and a flower scroll in the lower, it looks most effective painted a light olive green. The forecourt of the pavilion is laid around an octagonal star, which is formed by small grey pebbles on yellow sandstone.

Villa Alejandra, Acapulco

Tetelpa, Mexico City

Through this high, carved stone arched gate, one enters the mysterious gardens of Dr. Mario Gonzalez Ulloa's development overlooking Mexico City. This, the best example of "Architecture of Demolition," has gathered together a most extraordinary medley of old stone facades, columns, balustrades and every sort of beautiful object of the stonemason's and ironmaster's art. The talent of Arquitecto Manuel Parra, Carlos Obregon and later of English artist John Beadle, have combined all these varied elements to create a place of magic.

Below: Villa del Sol, one of the many paths in Tetelpa which takes one nowhere, except to a romantic stroll into the past.

Probably once marking the entrance to a small farm, this lichen encrusted masonry gate stands alone in the countryside, inviting one to guess its past history.

Gracefully decayed, this walk, bordered by flower pots in the Jardin Borda in Cuernavaca, reminds one of its once glorious past during the reign of Emperor Maximilian in the mid-nineteenth century.

Jardín Borda, Cuernavaca

Delightfully accurate, this iron orchid set over the door shows the way to one of the botanical wonders of San Miguel de Allende—Mr. Dickinson's much admired orchid gardens.

Of severe geometrical simplicity, this wooden gate brings a modern touch to the otherwise colonial surroundings of the town. The tile overhang protects it from the weather.

Home of Sterling Dickinson   *Valle de Bravo, Mex.*

Cuernavaca

Through this unpretentious entrance to an orchard in an old Hacienda, one comes upon a world of well-organized planting of fruit trees and vegetables, yet such is the Mexican delight in enriching everyday existence that one finds it full of charming little walks and benches.

Square cut grey stone frames this simple and graceful stucco shell, greatly enhanced by the little angel below.

51

Home of Wolfgang and Gisela Karmeinsky

These samples of the ironmaster's craft show us different ways of working this metal. The gate in La Mansion Galindo opens into the main patio and in spite of its great height has succeeded in keeping a delicate lace-like appearance. In heavy contrast is the top of this garden gate in Tetelpa. Made of cast iron, its origin is probably some demolished great mansion on one of Mexico City's elegant avenues and dates from the Porfirian period.

Effectively sober, the design of this gate to a house in the fashionable Pedregal district in Mexico City shows a strong influence of early seventeenth century ironwork.

53

Cuernavaca

Brought to the New World by the Spaniards during the conquest of Mexico, iron soon lost its martial usage to assume domestic functions. Iron bars and grills traditionally protect the houses of Mexico and Spain. The zealously guarded secrets of working this metal were forbidden to the natives during colonial times. However, some of these skills must have seeped through to the very inspired native craftsmen.

The two gates shown here speak for themselves as superb examples of the ironmaster's art. Ironwork in Mexico is usually painted black; whether from tradition or lack of imagination is difficult to tell.

Mexico City

Most original, these whimsical stepping-stones cross the tranquil brook of Mrs. Boddy's back garden. They are made of large round cobble-stones mortared together to make them look like lily pads just emerging from the water sufficiently to provide a dry crossing.

Famous Mexican artist Feliciano Bejar introduces the use of millstones as a garden path in his Mexico City home. With him, art always finds ornamental uses for everyday objects, making his houses and gardens a delight.

Home of Feliciano Bejar

Home of Beryl Boddy

Opposite page:

From time immemorial, all manner of trees have been used to line avenues and walks. Strange to say, this has been less prevalent in Spain, which has traditionally provided so much inspiration for design in Mexico, than in France, Italy and England. Whatever its source, it is a marvelous idea to have trees or tall plants shading walks or opening up lovely vistas of the house as one approaches. These majestic cacti line the entranceway through a large and imaginatively landscaped garden near Cuernavaca. Bordering the edges of the road, small flowering shrubs in tones of purple and yellow do much to soften the sense of aridity that cacti so often suggest.

Home of Beryl Boddy

Home of Peter and Elisabeth Gerhard

Home of Peter and Elisabeth Gerhard

Roughly cobble-stoned, this narrow road meanders through the lush garden of Tepoztlán's loveliest home. The white-washed stuccoed columns and arches form a brilliant contrast with the grey stone pavement and luxuriant greenery.

More formal in design, the cobble-stones here are interspaced with brick to produce an interesting optical pattern. The small stone saint stands in a niche carved out of a thick adobe wall flanked by two rounded stone buttresses. The color scheme combines grey stone, mellow apricot walls and green foliage.

Home of Manuel and Teresa Barbachano Ponce

Another house and garden of great importance in San Angel is the home of Mr. and Mrs. Manuel Barbachano Ponce. At one time the country home of a Spanish viceroy, this house has undergone many alterations since that time. At the beginning of this century, it was acquired by the author's grandfather, Cecil O'Gorman, who furnished it with a veritable treasure hoard of antique furniture, paintings and ornamental objects. Incredibly, he managed to live in undisturbed peace through the Mexican revolution of 1910, protected by the Union Jack flying from the top of his house. The present owner has had it substantially enlarged and modernized, but the gardens remain essentially the same. This old stone and stucco gate was used to divide the garden from the orchard but is now merely an ornamental feature. The stairs leading up to it are built of hard stone squares interspersed with brick.

59

In this contemporary Mexican garden, the paths are formed by placing asymmetrical slates capriciously over a bed of small pebbles and bordering these paths with haphazardly planted cacti.

This graceful entrance to a house in Cuernavaca elegantly combines different architectural elements and succeeds in accomplishing a most attractive whole.

Home of Leonard and Reva Brooks

Cuernavaca

Former Convento of Ocuituco

A hidden treasure are these poetically crumbling stairs and mysterious wooden door in the *convento* of Ocuituco. Although long abandoned, this orchard still tells us of the once active friars who grew their fruit and vegetables here to the greater glory of God. The open arched window above served as a lookout and these *miradores* were always placed facing the loveliest vistas.

61

Transplanted from their place of origin in some great city mansion, these venerable stone stairs enhance the landscaping of the elegant development of Tetelpa. The semicircular flower bed in the foreground is planted with lavender and bordered with yellow and white sweet alyssum whose pale colors gently blend with the mellow old stone. The ground is paved with squares of grey stone alternating with squares of terra-cotta-colored brick.

Tetelpa, Mexico City

Museo ex-Hacienda San Gabriel de Barrera

Oasis de paz,
Ambiente de reposo,
Que al cuerpo das
    solaz
y al alma gozo.

Oasis of peace,
Wellspring of repose,
That gives the body
    ease
and joy to the soul.

More adequate words cannot be found to describe the extensive and luxuriant gardens of the Hacienda San Gabriel de Barrera. Looking down this majestic carved stone staircase stands the towering statue of St. Francis of Assisi, the patron saint of gardens and birds.

63

Home of Elton and Martha Hyder

Restaurant San Angel Inn

Effectively used, these nineteenth century inspired terra-cotta urns form a charmingly different balustrade in a San Miguel de Allende garden. Seen against the surrounding ivy, the colors of the urns and geraniums give warmth and gaiety to the otherwise formal landscaping.

Enclosing a small back patio, this *celosia* (trellis) is made by joining the terra cotta components to form this design.

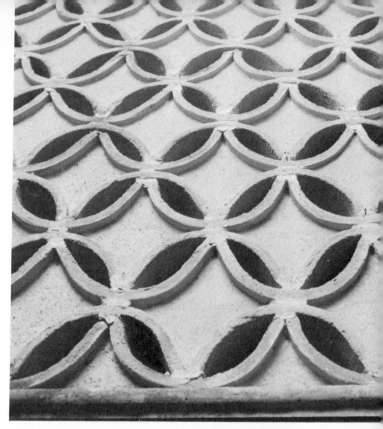

Home of Annette Potts

Home of Leonard and Reva Brooks

Both these *celosias* are extremely easy to make from readily available materials. The upper one is constructed of half circle commercially made tiles which resemble half an ordinary roof tile, thus the name *celosia de media teja.* Here they are fashioned into flowerlets by joining the tiles and filling in the appropriate spaces with mortar to form this design.

The lower one, of much simpler design, is built with ordinary construction bricks laid in this pattern and supported at the sides by a small reinforced concrete column. The whole is then stuccoed very roughly. The one depicted here is painted in a warm brownish pink and topped by a rather foxy looking stone lion.

Home of Ken Scott

Strikingly daring and original in concept, the home of designer Ken Scott in Cuernavaca is truly an experience. The garden is enclosed on all sides by towering walls that are covered by flowering vines and lush greenery. The swimming pool is tiled with black tiles, which retain the heat of the sun. The garden is formally laid out in symmetrical small flower beds. The view of the whole layout changes startlingly as one rises from one terrace to another, with a most impressive view from the highest level.

Home of José and Dolores Yturbe

The owner has only to walk out of his bedroom to be on this private terrace, where he can take a dip in a small tiled pool. The simple stucco pillars support two wooden beams for a pergola effect. The flower-filled terra cotta tub in the foreground actually was once used as such. The making of these tubs is a lost art since the natives now prefer to wash baby and clothes in ugly plastic counterparts. Therefore, they are highly prized nowadays and almost impossible to come by.

A strange mixture of eastern understatement and Mexican flora in the background gives this enclosed terrace a novel charm. The ground is paved with the largest made terra cotta squares, called *cuarterones*. Locally made, they are used throughout Valle de Bravo as both indoor and outdoor flooring.

67

Home of Robert Brady

Home of Marguerite Drewry

Built on a hillside, San Miguel de Allende's homes are a mountain goat's delight. The greatest variety of stairs are to be found here. The owner of this house, a sculptress, has taken this into account with grace and imagination. These stairs are made of brick laid on its short end and the stone wall itself serves as a balustrade and an ornamental feature. Into this wall, Mrs. Drewry has set copies of small archeological figurines which give it a light touch. The space under the stairs serves as useful storage for firewood and garden tools.

With his usual talent, Mr. Brady here again finds perfection. This archeological piece representing the *biznaga*, an edible cactus that grows wild in rocky areas, placed over the square stone pillar as a newel post, is most effective.

Forming one side of a mighty ravine, this many-terraced rose garden is accessible only by descending a very long and ingeniously built stairway at the bottom of which there is a beautifully tended expanse of lawn. The opposite side of the ravine is a masterpiece of landscape gardening. Mrs. Campbell amusingly recounts that she had to buy a goat for her gardener in order to design the paths by following it uphill.

Home of Feliciano Bejar

These semicircular steps, which form an amphitheater in Feliciano Bejar's romantic garden in Mexico City, serve a dual purpose. They actually are steps, but are also used as seats during the many performances which take place in this private open air theater.

Home of Feliciano Bejar

Most unusual, this rustic wall of loosely laid stones from various demolished homes forms an interesting background for this saint, who seems to miraculously perch in mid-air.

Peeking round the corner, a see-through iron and glass cat tells us of the joyous wit of its creator

Walking down these "demolition" granite stairs placed haphazardly among the greenery, the cat, like us, wonders where he'll get to. Mr. Bejar's compound has been created out of materials and objects from long demolished homes. The result of using these odds and ends as architectural features is novel and very striking.

Home of Feliciano Bejar

Home of Feliciano Bejar

Opposite page:

Cuernavaca's old-time charm, captured at its very best by the unique taste of the Leof's, shows everywhere in the classic touches that give this house and garden a sense of undisputed dignity and grace. These gently curving stairs take one to the many different garden levels. The balustrade is finished off by a molded cement handrail.

Below: One of the best uses for the magical *moneda* plant, a clinging vine with dark green leaves (Boston Ivy), is shown here as a cover for the risers of these garden steps.

74

Leaving space for narrow planters between each step gives this garden staircase a double purpose. The orange of the marigolds lightens the grey color of the slate.

Los Techitos, Acapulco

From this charming terrace high over the Bay of Acapulco, in one of the first homes built here, one can enjoy great privacy and a view of the ocean. The recess cut into the retaining wall in the background gives more space to place outdoor furniture.

Below: The use of the organ cactus as a boundary wall is widespread in Mexico and of very ancient origin. One has just to go off the road a mile or two in the dry areas of the country to see that all the native houses are surrounded by this enduring and most useful plant. It seems to thrive without water and it reproduces itself very easily by breaking off one of the small new sections and just sticking it into the ground. Certainly a hedge against the soaring costs of construction.

Home of Leonard and Reva Brooks

Home of Robert Brady

Combining several functions, this staircase leading up to the main entrance of Mr. Brady's house is at once a small fountain, an ornamental dividing wall and an approach in the grand manner of a Florentine villa.

In the foreground, the *moneda* and orchid-covered wall effectively shows up the simple fountain. The balusters are handmade of terra cotta, now very rare and difficult to find. Breaking the geometric simplicity of these steps, the Aztec figure is set into the low dividing wall. Pilli, the dachshund, sits pensively looking down.

Home of Robert Brady

The wall makes an interesting background for these beautifully shaped pots, once used in the old sugar mills near Cuernavaca to store molasses. They are now planted with large ferns.

Fountains as attractive as this one are to be found on almost every corner in San Miguel de Allende. Not only ornamental, they also supply much of the water needed by the native population for domestic chores. At Easter time, all the street fountains are decorated by the closest neighbors as altars to the Sorrowful Virgin Mary, with wheat sprouts, oranges and purple paper cut-outs.

Below and opposite page: Originally an old mill, this house in San Miguel de Allende was first remodelled by an American lady with a great penchant for things Italian. From its many terraces and different levels, it affords a marvelous view of the town and surrounding countryside.

The double brick stairs shelter between them, at the lowest level, a fountain in which water papyrus thrives. The original tower-like house and the high walls around it are almost entirely covered with a light purple trumpet vine intermingled with bougainvillea and pale blue plumbago.

San Miguel de Allende

Home of Peter Bubela

Las Hadas

In Las Hadas, a fairy-tale hotel and beach development on the Pacific coast near Manzanillo, these elegant stairs encompass a planter. A small village in itself, the hotel is an interesting combination of Moorish and Mediterranean-inspired architecture in which no luxury has been spared. The sight of the fantastic white-washed buildings surrounded by lush tropical vegetation against the sparkling blue of the sea is indeed breathtaking.

Loado seas Señor por la hermana Agua
La cual es muy util, humilde, alegre, preciosa
*   y casta.*

Blessed be thou, my Lord, for Sister Water,
Who is useful, humble, happy, precious and
   chaste.

So St. Francis of Assisi described water and so man from time immemorial has eulogized this precious element.

Opposite page:

This, perhaps the most beautiful fountain in Mexico, is built in the patio of the eighteenth century Casa del Risco in Mexico City's San Angel district. The towering central niche is flanked on both sides by two niches of smaller dimensions. These are formed by the gracefully descending sculptured walls on both sides. In these two lateral recesses, huge Chinese porcelain urns stand on bases. The central niche is extremely intricate in composition and is itself divided into many little niches. The whole fountain is surmounted by a glazed, polychromed ceramic figure. The water falls from a small basin under this niche into the large one in the foreground. This masterpiece was created from a combination of mother of pearl shells, left over crockery from several handpainted Limoges, Meissen, Porcelain des Indes and Chinese sets of dishes and fragments of mirrors. Only in the hands of an inspired artist could this strange combination have been transformed into sheer magic.

Casa del Risco, Mexico City

In the center of a now abandoned stable yard, this gracefully decaying masonry wellhead still serves as a source of water for the native population of a nearby village. On both sides of the well are storage tanks which are used as drinking troughs for cattle, to wash clothes and bathe in. Around these wellheads the scene is often most amusing, as all these activities go on at the same time amid much prattling, laughing and screams of irate children, who, like children everywhere, hate to take baths.

Opposite page:

Four fancifully carved stone rainspouts show the craftsman's talent for turning necessities into objects of beauty. Rainspouts are usually placed on the street facades of colonial style buildings to drain off the roofs and assist in the further drenching of the passerby. In dry parts of the country, these rainspouts pour into patios where the water is stored in reservoirs during the dry season.

Marfil, Gto.

This small eighteenth century reservoir on the road to Marfil in the State of Guanajuato gives lasting evidence of the great tradition that the people of Mexico have of transforming everyday necessities into sheer beauty. The *Presa de los Santos* stands alone and ignored by the roadside. Erosion and time have taken their toll of the beautifully carved statues of saints and of the Virgin of Guadalupe. The sight of the still water in the middle of the dry surrounding countryside makes it seem an oasis of peace and coolness. Pepper trees and willows, taking advantage of the nearness of the water, grow to great heights.

A charming conceit of the builder of this dam is the inscribed stone which reads, "José Alejandro Durán was the master mason. It was finished in November of the year 1778."

Framed by feathery leaves of a jacaranda and a nearby cactus, this statue of one of the saints on the dam's wall stares silently into space.

Ex-Hacienda de San Miguel Regla

Massively built of stone, these buildings of the once silver refining Hacienda of San Miguel Regla stand in the middle of an ornamental lake. The dam that contained the water was destroyed during the revolution of 1910 and these constructions have been flooded since then.

This beautiful stone bridge is part of the old hacienda, which has now been converted into an attractive hotel.

Opposite page: A vine-covered, European looking little house, approached by an arched bridge, stands as a garden folly in the center of this placid lake in the former Hacienda of San Miguel de Mendocinas.

Ex-Hacienda de San Miguel de Mendocinas

86

Home of Xavier Barbosa

Three different uses of water as an ornamental feature are seen here.

In a ranch in San Miguel de Allende, this rectangular reflecting pool breaks the symmetry of the pavement around it. It is filled by the overflow of the small carved stone basin. Rising beside it, the century plant flower has grown to a incredible height.

Home of Helen Ford

In Mrs. Helen Ford's unusual Cuernavaca home, water in itself is the central motif of the patio. A high wall with a green glazed tile shell niche makes a striking background for an antique fountain center from which water spills into the large, square, ornamental pool.

Below: Famed designer Arturo Pani can even improve on nature. Much thought has been given to the design of this seemingly simple little pond to make it a charming feature of his garden in Cuernavaca.

Home of Arturo Pani

This sparkling little brook refreshes and brightens Mrs. Boddy's lovely garden.

Taking full advantage of Cuernavaca's marvelous resources and renowned climate, the owner of this splendid mansion has done wonders with his large and beautiful grounds. As one approaches the level on which the house and pool are built, a brook overflows from a high rock, forming a small natural pool much enjoyed by the feathered creatures seen here. A great variety of plants border its banks, making it resemble an ancient Chinese print come to life.

Home of Beryl Boddy

Home of Alexander Kirkland

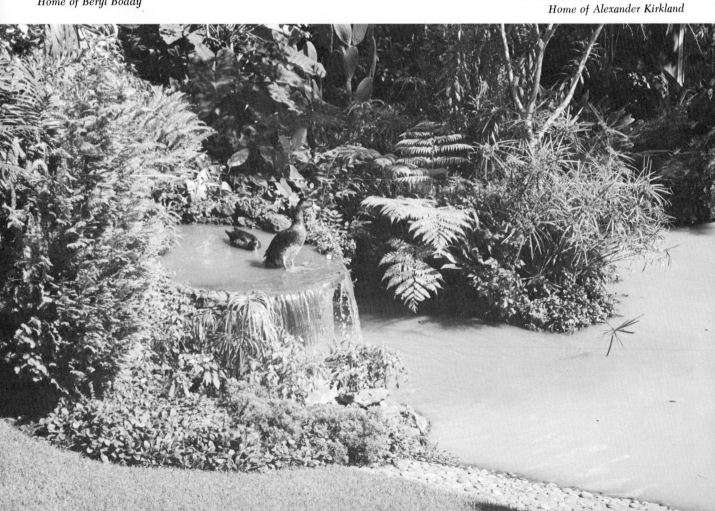

Home of the Marquis and Marquise de la Roziere

Touchingly tender, this little bronze child stands in the center of a circular fountain in a perfectly tended French style garden in San Angel. Small blue daisies grow around the edge of the fountain.

Home of Marcelo and Angela Javelly

Overgrown, secret and haphazardly planted, this old Coyoacán garden makes a perfect setting for the simple low fountain. The delicate sculpture of the dove is the work of well-known sculptress Angela Gurría.

91

Home of Olga Dominguez

Since ancient times, sculptural elements have been traditionally used as spouts to fill fountains and to give play and liveliness to water. In Mexico, the use of stone carvings for this purpose has prevailed since the time of the Spanish colony. The three examples depicted here fulfil this function most delightfully.

Above: Sitting on the edge of a circular fountain is this copy of an eighteenth century carved stone swan.

The dog in the photograph at left is a detail from a fountain in the center of Queretaro's loveliest square. From the fountain rises a rectangular pillar which is surmounted by a statue of the Marquéz de la Villa del Villar (for whom the square was once named). Dressed in full eighteenth century costume, he sports a wig, tricorn and sword. At his four sides, his faithful hunting dogs spout water into the fountain's basin.

Queretaro

This almost unrecognizable, cozy-looking lion is one of four that fill the fountain of the abandoned *convento* of Ocuituco in the State of Morelos.

Copied from an urn in the Palace of Versailles, this remarkable carved center stone is used as a fountain spout. The stone carver's art and attention to detail are most apparent in the fact that the face has truly European features and beautifully worked hair.

Home of David Brucilovsky

Ocuituco, Morelos

San Miguel de Allende

94   Of neo-classic inspiration, this street fountain graces a
corner in San Miguel de Allende and has the lovely name of
Fuente del Golpe de Vista.

These three sad looking tigers live up to the childrens' tongue twister that inspired their owner's fancy. *Tres tristes tigres tragaron tres tristes trigos.* Try saying it fast a few times. (Three sad tigers swallowed three sad blades of wheat.)

Sitting on their stone ledge overlooking a square tiled fountain in the sunny entrance patio of the Rancho San Joaquin, they look almost domesticated against the high white wall behind them.

Home of Antonio and Francesca Saldivar

Home of Maximilian and Elena Michel

◁

Because of their ornamental and practical value, fountains are found in almost all patios and gardens in Mexico. This one, designed by Arquitecto Alejandro von Wuthenau for his daughter's home, combines colonial charm with an unusual Italian feeling.

▷

Tiled in blue and white antique talavera tiles and now in use as a planter, this simple little fountain breaks the somewhat austere line of the beamed ceiling above it.

Home of Stewart and Alys Cort

Unlike the traditional fountains which one always finds placed in the center of patios, these four different fountains share something in common. They are garden fountains. Truth-fully, the two carved of stone either came from a patio or at least they were inspired by it.

Home of Inez Havermale

96

Home of Jaume Ribas

One gets a feeling of freedom and lightheartedness to see them used in the midst of unorthodox surroundings. In all of them the water spills over into the lower basins from a carved stone center, but otherwise each one has its own distinctive character.

Las Mañanitas, Cuernavaca

Of smaller dimensions and also placed in a garden, this circular fountain topped by a glass sphere enhances the entrance to a lovely Coyoacán home. The lower basin gives the dog a cooling drink while the higher one serves as a birdbath.

Home of José and Dolores Yturbe

Home of Jaume Ribas

At the entrance of the Yturbe's forecourt in Valle de Bravo, this understated rectangular reservoir also lets the dog have a drink.

98

This classically shaped little grey stone fountain-cum-birdbath is a charming idea for a small patio or garden.

Inspired by an oriental garden, this quiet retreat offers a feeling of peace and serenity. Encircling the birdbath, the slate border is raised to become a sitting area without losing its continuity.

Home of Leonard and Reva Brooks

Home of Harold and Frances Campbell

Home of Peter and Elisabeth Gerhard

Unassuming and simple, this circular fountain is built of masonry and tiled inside and out. The exterior design is formed by interspacing ceramic tiles in the stuccoed surface.

Below: A traditional low, carved stone fountain such as is found in many of Mexico's provincial public squares, is the main decorative feature in this sunny patio of a San Miguel de Allende home. Most unusual are the outdoor shell niches, which provide a perfect space for a beautiful fern or potted plant.

Home of Charles and Jinx Pratt

Museo ex-Hacienda de San Gabriel de Barrera

A true gem of an idea for a small area, this enchanting little stone fountain stands in a circular planter filled with violets. The basin is filled by the water spilling gently from the carved bouquet of roses.

101

Drawing by John Beadle

Home of Jack and Muriel Wolgin

With the lush Cuernavaca vegetation for a background, this splendid antique fountain glorifies the upper level of the Wolgins' garden. A Florentine statue of a boy holding a dolphin endows it with grace and tenderness. The custom of placing flowerpots around fountains is widespread and traditional. Ferns, geraniums and *permanentes* (impatiens) are year-round favorites.

Descending from this upper level through a delicate wrought iron gate, the black-tiled swimming pool looks most inviting. In the background and forming part of the pool itself, stands a raised platform with another smaller fountain at its center, topped by an identical Florentine statue which carries the motif of the upper fountain onto this level. Four rams' heads of carved stone continuously spout into the swimming pool.

Opposite page:

The simple lines of this swimming pool do nothing to distract one's attention from the stunning background provided by the arched facade of the house. The combination of the light ochre of the walls with the pale grey stone arches and the limpid blue of the water makes one feel one is in a magnificent Mediterranean villa. Placed exactly in front of the center arch, the small reflecting pool adds to this illusion. The intricate design of the pavement is a mosaic formed by river pebbles and white marble chips. The bottom of the reflecting pool is lined with blue and off-white ceramic tiles. Four little carved stone doves drink from the central birdbath topped with a blue and white glazed ceramic ornament.

Home of Alexander Kirkland

Where two massive stone garden walls meet, this unusual double shell niche makes a most impressive and eye-catching feature. The eighteenth century figure is of French origin. From the lower shell, the water falls into the semi-circular swimming pool. Altogether, an interesting use of a space usually wasted.

Home of the Marquis and Marquise de la Roziere

This circular tiled fountain in a patio of the Restaurant San Angel Inn is most unusual. Three large ceramic pots overflow into the tiled basin.

Restaurant San Angel Inn

Casa de Mara   *Home of Inez Havermale*

Two different types of carved stone fish, always great favorites as water spouts.

The small back garden is practically all taken up by the swimming pool, into which water gushes through this handsome Metepec earthenware sun. The low ornamental wall as well as the rim of the pool are tiled with a combination of chrome yellow and orange ceramic tiles, interspaced by deep blue stars on an oyster white background.

Home of Robert Brady

Home of Peter and Elisabeth Gerhard

To the lush vegetation and impressive natural setting of this garden,
the simple free-form swimming pool imposes a quiet restraint.

Home of María de la Luz von Wuthenau

The placing of these two stones and the feathery papyrus add
ornamental interest to this small swimming pool in Tepoztlán.

Outstandingly simple and most effective, this octagonal pool unifies the diverse architectural elements around it.

Home of Michael and Nicolette Possenbacher

Jardín Borda, Cuernavaca

Time has long passed by and forgotten this delicate little stone bird in the center of a fountain in the old Borda Gardens.

Home of Annette Potts

This stone urn piled high with fruit stands invitingly in a Cuernavaca swimming pool.

110

Home of Stewart and Alys Cort

The outdoor life of the owners revolves around these two attractive swimming pools. In Cuernavaca, the Corts' pool is well placed in the center of the lawn dividing the main house from the guest quarters. Marking its four corners, clumps of magenta and deep red dwarf bougainvillea give it a touch of glowing color.

Below: A romantic view of San Miguel de Allende in the background gives this sparkling pool a spectacular setting. On a lower level, a sundeck enjoys an even better view.

Home of Karl Eric Noren

Villa Alejandra, Acapulco

Villa Alejandra is the romantic name of one of Acapulco's most beautiful mansions. Set into acres of lush tropical gardens, the house escapes the rigors of the heat and is cooled and shaded by palms of all kinds. Tall coconut palms grow on the beach as well as in the gardens. The huge palapa on the beach

is used not only as a refuge from the sun, but also for beach parties. The long, irregular swimming pool is accessible from several covered loggias furnished in Tahitian style. The combination of brilliant red and white covered cushions with the dark green of the areka palms make these loggias glow like enchanted caves.

Villa Alejandra, Acapulco

Fun and sun in Acapulco are amply provided by the luxurious Acapulco Princess Hotel. Water cascades from man made waterfalls into two huge pools, providing a constant flow of fresh, clear water for the guests to swim in. All manner of tropical plants have been used in the masterly landscaping of the extensive grounds.

This unique scallop-shaped swimming pool in the garden of a villa in Acapulco seems to be rising out of the sea. The small shell at its apex is a charming duplication of the design of the pool. *Below:* A free-form pool makes imaginative use of a very small space on a terrace overlooking Acapulco Bay.

Los Techitos, Acapulco

Extensive fresh water swimming pools delight the guests of the Hotel Las Hadas, who can find shelter from the tropical sun and enjoy exotic drinks in these half-submerged bars covered by palapa roofs.

Two examples of famous sculptor Victor Salmones' life-like bronzes are beautifully placed in his Acapulco garden. On a sandstone rock, the little boy is busily concentrating on building a sand castle.

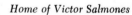

Home of Victor Salmones

116

Las Hadas

Also on a jutting sandstone rock on the beach below the house, this young man seems ready to step through the delicate frame into the sea in search of deeper dimensions.

An excellent copy of a double-tailed stone mermaid from the house of the Counts of Santiago de Calimaya (now the Museum of the City of Mexico) graces this tiled fountain. The lower basin is filled by the overflow from the upper bowl under the sculpture. Mermaids are a great source of inspiration to native craftsmen. The best known are the brilliantly colored Metepec figures which always play a mandolin to bewitch listeners with their siren song.

Opposite page: From earliest times in Mexico, plants, trees and flowers have been much venerated and cultivated, not only for their fruits but for their ornamental value. An eyewitness describing Moctezuma's garden at Oaxtepec (near Cuernavaca) said: "The gardens measured two leagues in circumference. In the middle ran a river, its banks shaded by the growth of many trees. Here and there were resting places with gardens of many different kinds of flowers and fruits. There were buildings, seed beds, fountains and scattered among the rocky cliffs, which were decorated with carvings, were arbors, chapels, lookouts and stairways cut into the very rock."

This Mazahua Indian woman is taking her offering of white, waxy *floripondios* (angel's trumpet) to present at the church of the Black Christ in Valle de Bravo on the day of the biggest fiesta.

118

Lovely and serene, this small river runs shaded by the ancient water cypresses on its banks.

Left and opposite page:

The amate is one of the most distinctive and beautiful trees that grow in hot climates in Mexico. Belonging to the fig (*ficus*) family, it starts to grow supported by a host tree which it finally envelops and destroys. Thus its native name of *matapalo*. Its roots take hold of old walls and foundations, becoming integrated with the building. It is a wonderful sight to see these light yellow trunks growing out of old, abandoned constructions. The natives of the state of Guerrero use its bark to make a fragile kind of paper on which they paint brightly colored scenes of everyday life in their villages.

Home of Beryl Boddy

Amidst these outcrops of volcanic rock, the fine lawns alternate with a well-chosen variety of cacti, trees, plants and shrubs to give this garden a very interesting style of its own.

Home of Harold and Frances Campbell

The kiss of the sun for pardon,
The song of the birds for mirth.
One is nearer God's heart in a garden
Than anywhere else on earth.

So reads a small plaque set into a wall of an impressive garden in Mexico City. The house high above faces this ravine, which has been beautifully landscaped and planted with a great variety of shrubs, flowering plants and trees.

A wide-eyed little stone figure sitting on its bed of *cortina* (ice plant) and geraniums seems to be waiting for something with infinite patience.

123

Home of Robert Brady

With the delightful name of *monstera deliciosa,* the *piñanona,* best known and most popular as an indoor plant, also grows to great heights in shady outdoor places. Planted in corridors and other covered areas, directly in the ground or in large flower pots, it is to be found in a great number of Mexican homes.

Home of Edmundo O'Gorman

Home of Harold and Frances Campbell

Home of Jack and Muriel Wolgin

A lovely mass of the succulent *echeveria* looks very much like a bouquet of green roses.

This mixture of succulents and Swedish ivy grows out of crevices in a low volcanic rock garden wall. Behind it grow white and pink azalea bushes and a loquat tree. The *nispero*, as it is called in Spanish, was imported from Japan, where it is also highly prized for its exotic-tasting fruit.

Home of Annette Potts

House in Cuernavaca

Home of the Marquis and Marquise de la Roziere

The most widely used plant to cover every kind of surface is the marvelous vine called *moneda* (Boston ivy). Walls, stair risers, roofs, columns and urns all wear its green mantle. Although it grows in other places also, it is in Cuernavaca where the *moneda* achieves unsurpassed glory. It clings so tenaciously to the surfaces it covers that it is very difficult to dislodge. It continues to reproduce itself by a process of self-grafting, so that one plant rooted in the soil is sufficient to cover a very large area.

Home of Milton and Sabina Leof

Cacti and succulents are found in great numbers in the extensive arid regions of Mexico. These plants have now made their appearance in contemporary gardens. In colonial patios, cacti were never tolerated, since these exotic and usually prickly plants were much at odds with what was thought decorative and proper. It is only in recent years that it has been fashionable to have them in gardens and pots.

A succulent that grows in many gardens in Mexico, especially in the Pedregal volcanic lava gardens, is this *euphorbia* (spurge).

In the large nursery of Los Viveros in Mexico City, these babies are waiting to be adopted and taken home to fill a rock garden.

Hacienda de Cortez, Atlacomulco

Los Viveros de Coyoacán

Twin Dolphin Hotel, Baja California

In the Twin Dolphin Hotel in Baja California these Stenocerus cacti are not only beautifully placed, but seem to thrive in the desert garden.

Below: These dark green columnar organ type cacti are topped by their reddish or pink bell shaped flowers.

Helen O'Gorman is well known as a botanist and as the creator of these enchanting flower paintings taken from her book, *Mexican Flowering Trees and Plants,* now unfortunately out of print and extremely difficult to find.

She first came to Mexico during the Second World War and became a friend of famous muralist Diego Rivera, who encouraged her to develop her painting talent and introduced her to Juan O'Gorman, also a prominent muralist, to whom she is married.

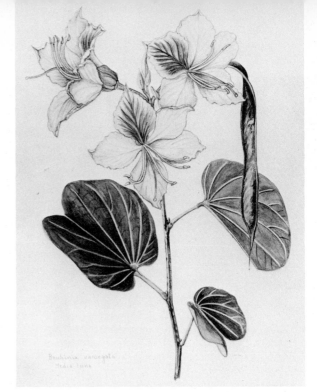

Orchid tree

Imported originally from India or China, the delicate mock orchid tree (*media luna*) grows beautifully in Cuernavaca gardens. Its leaves are veined and the delicate flowers are a combination of lavender and purple.

Jacaranda

Found everywhere in Mexico, this much-loved tree, the Jacaranda, not only grows in gardens, but lines many streets and avenues. When they are in bloom, they are indeed a breathtaking sight, especially when combined with masses of purple bougainvillea. The flowers wilt and fall soon after they bloom, covering the ground under the trees with a carpet of violet-blue. The leaves are finely cut, making the tree itself look like a large, delicate fern.

Magnolia

The magnolia was one of the highly prized ornamental trees of the royal gardens of the Aztecs. It was greatly appreciated by the natives for the sweet, spicy odor of its blossoms, a single flower being considered sufficient to perfume a palace. The waxy white flowers of this large evergreen tree appear from May to July. The native name, *yoloxochitl* (heart flower), was given to it because the unopened buds resemble a heart.

130

Copa de Oro

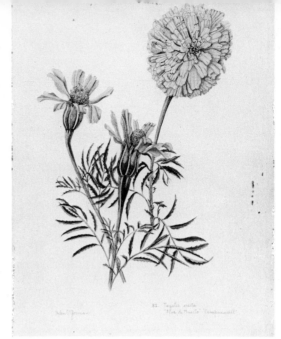

Aztec Marigold

Often cultivated to cover garden walls, to frame the openings into patios or to hang from pergolas, this clambering shrub is present in many of the older patios and gardens. The leaves are dark green and lustrous, the flower, as its name in Spanish indicates (*copa de oro*), is golden yellow and most fragrant, especially in the early morning.

Big yellow-headed annuals with delicate leaves, marigolds (*flor de muerto*) have been connected in Mexico with religious rites since ancient times. Specially grown in vast quantities for the celebration of All Souls' Day (*Dia de los Muertos*), they are taken by the natives to cemeteries as offerings for the dead and placed in glowing bouquets on the graves.

Flame Vine

Bougainvillea

A great favorite in warm climates is this delicate vine called *llamarada* (flame vine), with its clusters of orange, trumpet-like flowers. Covering the many stone walls or mixed with plumbago and bougainvillea, it presents a glorious sight.

The crowning glory of the Mexican garden is the bougainvillea. Bearing glowing purple, dark red or amber yellow flowers in great profusion, it covers walls, pergolas, tiled roofs, and takes over trees to pour forth a cascade of brilliant color that delights the eye the whole year round.

131

Home of Bob and Nina Schalkwijk

Against the dramatic crags of Tepoztlán, these two gardens show a great variety of plants and shrubs that do so well in the semi-tropical climate that they have to be cut back constantly so that the gardens don't become a jungle.

Opposite page: The former Hacienda of San Gabriel de Barrera has one of the few gardens in Mexico designed as an imitation of a formal European garden. Surrounding a bronze urn placed in the center as a focal point, the symmetrical flower beds are planted with rose bushes and ornamental cabbages. Time-worn brick paths separate these flower beds.

Home of Peter and Elisabeth Gerhard

Museo ex-Hacienda de San Gabriel de Barrera

For the native population of Mexico, flowers have two important uses. One is to decorate altars in churches and in their own homes and the other is to take them as offerings for the dead to the cemeteries on the Day of the Dead. This day, November 2nd, is a great fiesta in Mexico, and although it takes place in the cemeteries, it is not a sad affair but a happy and colorful one, the Mexicans being such gay souls. Picnics are eaten near the grave and the colorful sugar skulls and lambs, part of the offering, are eaten by children on the way home.

Cemetery Valle de Bravo

Toluca Market

It is considered a great compliment to be given a sugar skull with one's name on it. Recently, in places like Cuernavaca and San Miguel de Allende, it is possible to find such un-Mexican names as Edgar or Susan, which delights foreigners who felt sadly left out.

Restaurant San Angel Inn

An interesting use for these old tree trunks is to convert them into planters. Hollowed out, filled with soil and then covered with wire netting to hold the plants in place, this trunk is planted with fuchsia above while a sedum hangs at the sides. The large tree trunk at right makes a natural and very attractive container for a dwarf bougainvillea in a garden in Cuernavaca.

136

The *pirul* (pepper tree) is found not only in the countryside, where it is an intrinsic part of the Mexican landscape, but also in gardens in Mexico City. This fine example shades the forecourt of a home in the elegant Pedregal district.

Home of Ignacio and Guadalupe Iturbe

The back wall of the Parroquia of San Miguel de Allende has a charming old world flavor. The brick trellis balustrade is covered with blue plumbago mixed with pink climbing geraniums and yellow jasmin. The fountain in the center of the cobble-stoned patio is filled with tall papyrus.

Former Convento of Angahua

Carved on a stone base in an old building is this charming floral motif, above which the crosses are intertwined with cords ending in acorns.

Home of Ken Scott

Home of Eric and Pauline Guernier

On the highest wall of Ken Scott's tower-like house in Cuernavaca this variety of cacti and succulents seems to reach out into the sky.

In the well-tended garden of a modern home in the Pedregal, this large jacaranda, surrounded by attractive planting, gives shade as well as its magic violet-blue flowers in the spring.

Casa de las Campanas

140   The imaginative use of the quatrefoil shape as a garden bench encircling an orange tree looks very inviting in this old city garden. It is a widespread custom to surround trees with low walls called *arriates* on which flower pots are placed to give added color. This one is built of masonry, the cornice formed by overlapping and hand-shaping three layers of *ladrillo,* terra cotta floor tile.

As in all colonial country houses, behind the main building one comes upon the orchard, which here has a circular clearing with an old stone fountain in its center. This space is often used for outdoor theatrical performances in the warm months before the rainy season. Rounding off this area are several masonry benches made in sections to form the circle, guarded by stony-faced, primitively carved saints.

Below: Clivias, with their long dark green leaves and their clusters of brilliant orange flowers, thrive in flower pots or in the ground away from direct sunlight. They are ideal plants for the more shaded places in gardens and shelters.

Home of Harold and Frances Campbell

141

Home of Bob and Nina Schalkwijk

Under the shade of the very tall *fresno* (white ash tree), masses of pink and white azaleas bloom almost all the year round. The light yellow wall of the studio in the background is covered by a pink trumpet vine.

Opposite page:

The custom of placing sculpture in gardens and patios for merely ornamental purposes, although already existing in colonial times, really gained popularity from the middle of the nineteenth century. No doubt this was due to a strong French influence prevalent in Mexico at that time.

Home of Robert Brady

In the forecourt of a house in Cuernavaca, this unusual piece of sculpture lurks among the greenery. Its owner calls it "The Dictator." Below him, the lion holding a heraldic device probably topped the newel post of a grand staircase.

143

Home of Federico Patiño

Messengers of good tidings, angels have always been a great subject for garden sculpture. Posing on columns, inside niches, over doors and as the centers of fountains, these heavenly beings inspire many a craftsman.

Standing on a tall stone column in a patio in Coyoacán, this little angel seems to wave at the earthlings below.

144

Home of Raoul and Carolina Fournier

Hotel la Mansión Galindo

These three stone denizens of the celestial host really represent the archangel St. Michael, often invoked to guard entrances from evil, a function this saint is well known for.

145

The king of beasts, symbolically used to guard and give a feeling of strength and power, is another favorite subject for outdoor sculpture. A native interpretation gives this lion a distinctly Pre-Columbian appearance, while the smaller one below him, more Spanish in appearance, smiles happily.

Las Hadas

Home of Xavier Barbosa

146

Home of Raoul and Carolina Fournier

Ably portraying the outstanding characteristics of the lion, this noble stone beast suns himself in the Fournier's garden in Mexico City.

Age and weather have taken their toll on this old lion guarding the entrance to an abandoned *convento*.

A strong archaeological influence gives indigenous characteristics to this lion at the entrance to a garden in La Mansion Galindo. Lions were unknown in Mexico until the knowledge of them was brought over by the Spaniards in the sixteenth century.

Below: Surrounded by balustrades and demolition stones, this powerful, life-like stone lion shows off the skill of its creator.

"Casas Coloniales", San Miguel de Allende

In contrast to the lions shown on the preceding pages, this beautiful pair of lambs look meek and gentle. The lamb, too, was introduced to Mexico by the Spanish during the Colony. Associated with the "Lamb of God," they can usually be found in churches and *conventos* but are rarely found in private homes. The two French-inspired urns shown here are excellent copies made by skilled San Miguel de Allende artisans.

149

Las Hadas   *Coyoacán, Mexico D.F.*

The sun in Mexico is used everywhere as a decorative motif, probably a tradition inherited from the earliest native cultures that worshipped the sun. These two suns, carved out of hard grey stone, add warmth to the exterior whitewashed walls.

150

Tetelpa, Mexico City

An ancient device for telling time between sunrise and sunset, sundials have been in use from time immemorial. The sundial carved on the face of the stone sun combines both ornament and usefulness. Two examples of colonial sundials, one is placed over a tiled rooftop and the other in the middle of a garden.

Hacienda de Cortez, Atlacomulco

Tlaxcala

Archeological sculpture can be displayed to
great advantage in gardens where, surrounded
by nature, it acquires a magnificence that
often seems to be lacking when placed in-
doors. This is especially the case with sculptural pieces that were meant to be under the
open sky.

Home of Manuel and Teresa Barbachano Ponce

This Mayan stela, commemorating a long forgotten event of great significance, rises from its base, made out of an old colonial fountain, now used as a planter. Intricately carved stone stelae several meters high were placed by the Maya of the classical period in their city squares to mark great events or honor illustrious men.

153

Home of Manuel and Teresa Barbachano Ponce

In the same garden, this classical Maya head is also displayed to great advantage using an old tree trunk as a base and surrounding it with azaleas and flowering acanthus. The fantastic headdress depicted here was the Maya noble's chief crowning glory. Nowhere have these feather marvels ever been surpassed.

House in San Miguel de Allende

Opposite page: An ornamental inspiration is the use of this thick wall in a garden in Coyoacan. The arch around the niche is made with alternating sections of differently worked and colored volcanic rock. The russet tones of the stone and interior of the niche look very attractive against the whitewashed wall.

Home of Peter Schalkwijk

Tetelpa, Mexico City

Tethering rings, like this little cast iron horse's head, were used to tie up horses in Mexico from the arrival of the Spaniards to the advent of the automobile. They can be found set into walls in all manner of buildings. This one in San Miguel de Allende adds a charming touch to a traditional facade.

This French-inspired urn crowns a pillar in Tetelpa, very much forming part of the architectural style of the house in the background.

156

This primitive angel brings to mind the paintings of well-known artist Chucho Reyes, who through his art infused color and grace into his naive style of painting.

Another primitive interpretation of a statue, copied from an existing one in the famous English garden at Sissinghurst, this Aztec-looking sphinx sits on the stone balustrade of a garden in San Miguel de Allende.

Home of Federico Patiño

House in San Miguel Allende

Waiting to be discovered in an over-grown garden are these two romantically placed sculptures. A delicate stone goat peers out appealingly from the tall flowering acanthus in Feliciano Bejar's garden.

Half man and half goat, Pan slumbers away, almost covered by wild grasses and flowers. The god of flocks and shepherds, he has long been a favorite subject for garden sculpture.

Home of Feliciano Bejar

159

Home of Robert Brady

Home of Cynthia Sarge...

Small, decorative stone figures, these enhance their surroundings. Stone finials have long been used on walls, stairs and over cupolas and fountains in colonial architecture. The name of the finials in Spanish is *piñas* (pine-apples), although they have very little to do with that fruit.

The dog sits begging hopefully at the entrance of a house, while the little stone elephant brings good luck to its owner's garden.

Home of Bob and Nina Schalkwijk

Former Convento of Yurir...

Home of Helen Henley

To support or carry is the function of this charming group. The eighteenth century French white stone monkey is actually a garden stool, but can also carry a tray or a flowerpot on its tasselled cushion.

Another stony-faced primitive, this figure proudly bears a flower pot. Its basket can also be filled with freshly cut flowers.

In the coolest places of corridors and arcades, carved stone shelves were placed to

Restaurant San Angel Inn

hold ceramic jars of lemonade or drinking water, living up to their name of *aguadores* (water bearers).

This caryatid is one of a pair that holds up a beam used as a garden shelf in Cuernavaca.

Home of Jesús and Yolanda Morales

Home of Rafael and Enriqueta Casasola

Home of Raoul and Carolina Fournier

Standing gracefully for no other purpose than to be ornamental, these four tall fluted stone columns with their intricately carved capitals give an old garden a romantic touch.

Placed on a primitive fluted half-column, this horse's head forms the charming newel post of a balustrade in a garden in the Pedregal.

Opposite page: Giving great importance to a corner in Mr. Barbachano's garden is a carved stone niche surrounded by flowering vines and pink azaleas.

Home of Manuel and Teresa Barbachano Ponce

163

Museo ex-Hacienda de San Gabriel de Barrera

Home of the Marquis and Marquise de la Roziere

This flower-like birdbath topped by a charming bronze statuette stands at the center of a French-style flower bed of clipped box in a formal garden.

St. Joseph presides over the entrance to San Gabriel de Barrera from a base set in an octagonal carved stone tub.

Opposite page: All manner of religious statuary is found in patios and gardens in Mexico, but none is a greater favorite than St. Francis of Assisi, always portrayed surrounded by birds to whom legend says he preached. Statues of St. Francis are carved of stone or wood and usually placed near fountains or birdbaths so that little birds may pay him a visit.

Home of Elton and Martha Hyder

Home of Xavier Barbosa

This little angel musician, found in the un-cultivated part of the Rancho San Joaquin, delights the rambler who discovers him. Dressed sometimes in a native interpretation of a Roman soldier's costume, angels were prime decorative subjects in the time of the Spanish Colony. Some of the most beautiful and colorful are to be found in the church of Tonantzintla near Puebla.

Splendidly carved is this unusual representation of the Holy Trinity. The sculptor took great pains to make them look as alike as possible. The Father has an all-seeing eye, the Son a Lamb of God and the Holy Ghost a Dove. Probably this piece was carved for the portico of a church, but in Mr. Clapp's colorful garden it looks blessedly happy.

Home of Oliver and Estelle Clapp

166

Home of Manuel and Teresa Barbachano Ponce

Restaurant San Angel Inn

Traditionally placed in the atriums of churches, stone crosses also adorn the gardens and patios of houses. Crosses like the large one seen here were put up by the priests to celebrate the ending of a successful mission to convert the natives.

167

Casa de las Campanas

Opposite page: Placed to great advantage in the garden of the O'Gormans is this modern stone sculpture of Angela Gurria's. Entitled *El Espejo* (The Mirror), it is a self-portrait of the sculptress.

Home of Juan and Helen O'Gorman

Home of Juan and Helen O'Gorman

Looking through their square windows, the children in this imaginative modern sculpture look perfectly contented. Partly covered with ivy and impatiens (an ever-flowering shade plant), Angela Gurria's work contrasts greatly with the rest of the house, built in sober colonial style.

At the entrance of the O'Gormans' garden in San Angel, this primitive hard stone sculpture, the work of Mardonio Magaña, captures the long suffering look one sees on the faces of many campesino women.

168

Opposite page: Seen from above, the Acapulco garden of sculptor Victor Salmones is utterly breathtaking. Many acres of steep, rock-covered ground terraced by a masterpiece of landscape engineering separate the house, built on an incredibly high site, from the beach below.

The brick-covered walks and steps leading to these terraces are designed so that at each level one finds a small garden with a fountain or one of Mr. Salmones' bronzes as the focal point. At no time are these terraces and different levels isolated from the whole; they all form part of the complete entity.

Lying in full view is a colossal bronze sculpture of "Aquarius." The original was commissioned by Metromedia for its headquarters in Los Angeles.

Home of Victor Salmones

House in Mexico City

A totally different concept, this amusing garden folly is a replica of a belltower. Standing in a square raised platform, it is one of Arquitecto Manuel Parra's more whimsical ideas.

Deep in thought, this "Shoeshine Boy," the work of talented
Helen Escobedo, strikes a contemporary note in the otherwise gentle,
English-style garden of her mother's house in San Angel.

Ruins of Palenque

To observe life around him has always been a great source of interest and amusement to man. Curiosity, scientific or merely human, has motivated this fascination since the earliest times. In Mexico, examples of this interest are to be found in many archeological sites.

Built in the purest style of the classic Maya period, the archeological site of Palenque gives testimony to the greatness of the Maya culture. This observation tower, or lookout, is still beautifully preserved.

Home of Robert and Violet Rice

174   A striking combination of terrace and mirador, this covered arcade is an extension of the
living room in the Rices' house in San Miguel

de Allende. Large flower-filled ceramic tubs
and pots form a colorful foreground for the
lovely view of the town.

Home of Robert and Violet Rice

Below: With her well-known green thumb, the English owner of this charming roof garden has accomplished wonders. Cypresses and orange trees actually grow in large masonry planters, and many varieties of potted plants and cooking herbs give it freshness and color. The pergola, covered with loosely tied bamboo, makes a rustic shelter.

Home of John and Sylvia Beadle

Home of Robert and Mary Buckner

Far from the noise of the street below, this tiled roof retreat is much used by its artist owner. Hot pink and red geraniums are planted in the raised planters, and carved stone finials give a touch of elegance to the curved wall behind them.

Below: At the end of the long avenue leading from the house, this amusing rotunda is a surprising find in the Mexican landscape.

Home of Xavier Barbosa

Casa del Inquisidor

This gem of a carved stone facade is one of the outstanding architectural treasures in San Miguel de Allende. Legend has it that it was once the house of the Inquisitor, but there is much doubt that the presence of such an official was ever required. To quote Mexican historian Francisco de la Maza, "Heresy was not a plant that flourished in the most Christian city of San Miguel." These beautiful, flower-laden balconies relieve the solid brown of the stone.

177

Museo ex-Hacienda San Gabriel de Barrera

House in San Miguel de Allende   *House in Guanajua*

Usually surrounded by carved stone frames, windows that give on to the street are traditionally barred with iron grilles. Shown here are three examples of the workmanship in iron and stone.

Home of Elton and Martha Hyder

Beautifully worked are the two railings guarding these interior balconies. Unfortunately, the art of casting iron is no longer practiced, so that the center section of the railing in the photograph below could not be equaled on the sides.

Home of Charles and Jinx Pratt

Drawing by John Beadle

Any house that is fortunate enough to possess a balcony on the street side has at its disposal a private, ringside seat from which can be observed the activities and fiestas going on below.

Used to support the balconies depicted here, these carved stone animals used as corbels are set into the wall. The balcony supported by the dogs is one of many stone carvings on the facade of the Casa de los Perros in San Miguel de Allende. The one held up by cats comes from a house in Queretaro.

"Casa Maxwell", San Miguel de Allende

House in Queretaro

181

House in Guanajuato

The sole attraction of this nineteenth century balcony is its unique cast iron railing. The grapevine sections frame the portraits of, perhaps, famous statesmen, or the owners or builders of the house.

Below and opposite page:
Another architectural charmer, this colonial house occupying a street corner in Queretaro is built of stone. The balcony, facade, is supported by finely carved stone corbels.

House in Queretaro

Casa de Correos, Guanajuato

Mineral de Cata, Guanajuato

Running along the whole length of the upper floor, this flower-filled balcony overlooks the square of a charming mining village. Performances of the Spanish Classical Theater often take place in this square. Like many railings in Spain, these have iron hoops to hold flower pots.

An extremely ornate shell that tops this carved stone frame and a unique wrought iron railing give a touch of elegance to the Post Office balcony in Guanajuato.

House in Zacatecas

House in Queretaro

Supported by carved corbels which appear to rest on the dentil cornice, this balcony runs around the upper part of the building. Of strong nineteenth century influence, the elaborate railing has a flavor of art nouveau.

These balconies in Queretaro demonstrate the classic simplicity of Spanish-inspired architecture of this period. An extension of the lower cornice forms the ledge of the balconies and supports the railings, which are adorned with brass knobs.

185

Cathedral of Cuernavaca

Opposite page:

Overlooking the vast garden of a house in Cuernavaca, this covered area is an ideal place from which to watch the sunset. The heavy master beam and double wood corbels are supported by antique fluted columns.

Home of Jack and Muriel Wolgin

House in Cuernavaca

The tradition of the mirador in colonial architecture was brought to Mexico by the Spaniards. They, in turn, had inherited this fascinating idea from the Moors.

From this massively built stone mirador, one gets a marvelous view of the city of Cuernavaca. The small arched balustrade is made of masonry with a carved stone cornice.

Combining a wide variety of architectural elements, the builder of this amusing house has given great importance to the mirador.

186

Tetelpa, Mexico City

The ledge that divides the two levels of this facade forms
a balcony beautifully guarded by a curved iron railing.

Towering above the surrounding countryside near Cuernavaca, this balcony commands an imposing view over the tops of the trees.

This mirador is an extension of a rooftop terrace, from which one gets an excellent view of the fantastically shaped crags that surround Tepoztlán.

Home of Edmundo O'Gorman

House in Tepoztlán

189

In a place where wood is abundant, the ornamental things that in other parts of Mexico are made of iron, are in Valle de Bravo made of wood, like the finely carved railings of these two balconies.

House in Valle de Bravo

House in Valle de Bravo

The rustic method of weatherproofing and protecting wood in Mexico is either to paint it with hot tar dissolved in kerosene, or to paint it with used car oil. This seems to work extremely well, as these outdoor wooden structures last forever in the very wet climate of Valle de Bravo.

A typical native town house, where the use of wood is much in evidence. The columns that support the tiled roof are carved tree trunks, the railing of the balcony is also made of wood. The lower part of these houses is usually taken up by business premises, while the owners live on the upper floors.

This amusing tin cut-out is the sign of the veterinarian's drugstore.   *Valle de Bravo*

House in Valle de Bravo

191

Valle de Bravo

In a more sophisticated and well-kept town house in Valle de Bravo, the unusual wrought iron gate gives an ornamental touch to the simplicity of the facade.

These blue and white tiled signs in Valle de Bravo often bear amusing names like this one meaning "Street of the Rats."

Home of Christopher and Mary King

Francisco Kalnay, an architectural designer of great imagination, was one of the first people to discover the beauty and possibilities of Valle de Bravo. An intensely versatile man, he adapted the prevalent style of construction in the town to the necessities of modern life without losing its spirit. His houses are usually placed in a way that gives them the best view of the lake.

These two houses show how nearly his designs follow the traditional pattern of construction while retaining a very personal charm.

House in Valle de Bravo

House in Valle de Bravo

During a recent remodelling, this house was given a contemporary version of the traditional balcony.

House in Valle de Bravo

Ingeniously built, this long terrace looks out over the lake, while the lower part is used as an open garage or to tie up horses. In the background is the huge rock that gives its name, *La Peña*, to this elegant subdivision of Valle de Bravo.

194

Charmingly simple, this roof garden is also a mirador, since it commands an all-round view of the lake and surrounding countryside of San Miguel de Allende. The large tree is a *pirul* (pepper tree), ever present in the Mexican landscape.

Surrounded by mellow stone walls, this many-terraced San Miguel garden affords a great sense of privacy and peace to its artist owners. George Anselevicius, a prominent U.S. architect, designed this garden, using the limited space to the utmost advantage, even to the extent of including a small swimming pool.

Home of Richard and Chantal Lusby

Home of Oliver and Estelle Clapp

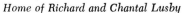

The colonial concept of the mirador is beautifully depicted here.
Through this double, arched opening, the monks of this *con-vento* were able to contemplate the passing of the centuries.

"Casa Maxwell", San Miguel de Allende

In order to complete the landscape designer's and architect's creation, much care and thought must be given to the lighting and furniture of a patio or garden. Fortunately, in Mexico, land of talented craftsmen, this presents no problem. Lace-like design gives this iron table and chairs an appearance of lightness which goes very well with the tasselled white cotton sun umbrella.

197

Casa de las Campanas

The park or garden bench also becomes an ornamental feature in these gardens.

An old wood bench is invitingly placed at the entrance to the Casa de las Campanas in Coyoacán. Mexican courtesy dictates that the caller, whatever his business, should never be kept standing.

Tetelpa, Mexico City

Below: To go with flamboyant style that characterizes the gardens of Tetelpa, this cast iron park bench was probably brought here from a provinical town square.

Opposite: Of French origin, this ornate garden bench shows four high reliefs of reapers in eighteenth century costume on the backrest.

Home of Jorge and Sara Larrea

Home of Sloane Simpson

Home of Edmundo O'Gorman

From the rustic simplicity of the rush-bottomed native chair to the sophistication of the wrought iron one on the opposite page, many styles are found, usually placed around tables in outdoor spaces. The interesting carved wooden chair *(below)* is painted in a combination of yellow and orange.

"Casas Coloniales", San Miguel de Allende

Home of Alexander Kirkland

Las Hadas

The trend in today's outdoor furnishing is to make furniture an integral part of the architectural whole. In this Cuernavaca garden, the long masonry bench is covered with white canvas cushions. An old millstone functions as a center table, with an antique pestle and mortar used as a decorative motif.

Home of Michael and Nicolette Possenbacher

Casa Emilia, Acapulco

Casa Emilia, Acapulco

Functional simplicity is the mood here. The side tables are partly covered with hand-painted blue and brown ceramic tiles to avoid staining the all-pervading whiteness. The thick, soft cushions are covered in a rough, ribbed cotton material of light brown and pale yellow stripes. The only strong touch of color is provided by the small objects on the tables. A ceramic base charmingly ornamented with fish and topped by a glass cover becomes a table, surrounded here by carved, natural wood color chairs.

Home of Rafael and Enriqueta Casasola

This set of wrought iron outdoor furniture is very delicate. The chairs have back rests and seats woven of plastic cord.

Below: Used as a garden table, this old cartwheel finds yet another way to be of use in the garden of a hacienda near Cuernavaca.

Hacienda de Cortez, Atlacomulco

204

Museo ex-Hacienda San Gabriel de Barrera

Tiled park and patio benches are very prevalent in Mexico. Here, in a beautiful old *convento*, they are most effectively placed around the fountain which is also tiled on the outside.

An old wooden carousel horse becomes an amusing ornament in a Hacienda arcade. These horses have now become collector's items The one here is especially attractive and well preserved.

205

Home of Peter and Elisabeth Gerhard

These four different versions of garden seats form part of the architectural whole. Behind these white masonry columns, the tiled bench and raised table spaces make an attractive seating arrangement.

Integrated with this planter, the stone ledge becomes a narrow seat.

206

This old garden seat gives the impression that, although the combination of ideas and materials is slightly disjointed, it all turned out surprisingly well.

An attractive touch is given to this window by the garden seat under it.

Tetelpa, Mexico City   *Restaurant San Angel Inn*

Casa del Arbol, Cuernavaca

Casa de las Campanas

House in Cuernavaca

House in Cuernavaca

In their different charming ways, these signs bearing the names of houses show the fantasy of their creators. Hand-painted on ceramic plaques and tiles, they give a touch of glowing color to the usually austere walls around them. The lower one, "Recreo 96," is a carved replica of a nineteenth century design, set over the door of a house in San Miguel de Allende.

Tetelpa, Mexico City

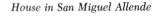
House in San Miguel Allende

Home of Robert Brady

Home of Annette Potts

Outstanding examples of metal craftsmanship, these three door knockers are found on the street doors of houses in Mexico. The ceramic plaques, originally from Guatemala, hide the electric bell buttons in their mouths. Door knockers and bells are usually placed very high up so that children are not tempted to ring or knock just for fun.

me of Milton and Sabina Leof   *Home of Olga Dominguez*   *Home of Maximilian and Elena Michel*

Home of Wolfgang and Gisela Karmeinsky

Home of Jack and Muriel Wolgin

Wrought iron is much used outdoors and several useful as well
as ornamental objects are made
from it. The two weather vanes
of different inspiration share the
page with a movable plant stand.

House in Mexico City

Las Hadas

Even the humble function of covering manholes is transformed into an art by these intricately designed covers.

Home of Alexander Kirkland

211

Home of Feliciano Bejar

Fascinating distortions are captured by this mirrored jar set in a balustrade in Feliciano Bejar's garden.

Opposite page:

Made originally to be carried in religious processions, these elaborate lanterns now adorn many gardens and patios. Either wired for electricity or bearing candles, their flickering light gives the final touch to houses built in colonial style. This large lantern in the shape of a cross is made of tin and glass.

Home of Elton and Martha Hyder

Home of the Marquis and Marquise de la Roziere

Home of Robert Brady　　　　　　　　　　　*Home of Annette Potts*

An interesting variety of wrought iron outdoor light fixtures (*faroles*) light up entrances, gardens and streets. All are held by brackets made of the same metal.

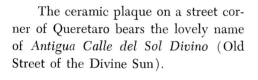
Home of Josue and Jaqueline Saenz

The ceramic plaque on a street corner of Queretaro bears the lovely name of *Antigua Calle del Sol Divino* (Old Street of the Divine Sun).

Home of Rafael and Enriqueta Casasola

Home of Annette Potts

The extensive imagination of the craftsman has made light an unending subject for his art. Cut out of tin and
then enamelled in a fresh combination
of yellow, white and green, this chan-
delier and flower ornament add a touch
of gaiety to an open air living room in
Cuernavaca.

Home of Jack and Muriel Wolgin

Home of Sloane Simpson

Whether as wall brackets, hanging or standing, these iron light fixtures solve problems of decoration concerning outdoor lighting.

Hacienda de Cortez, Atlacomulco

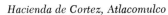

217

Tetelpa, Mexico City

This griffin-inspired iron street lamp illumi-
nates the gardens of Tetelpa. Probably cast
during Porfirio Diaz's regime, when all things
French were in style, it is a perfect reproduc-
tion of a European model.

Home of Helen Henley

These cleverly designed night lights mingle unobtrusively with the garden vegetation. The upper one, made of tin and painted white, resembles a flower.

Hacienda de Cortez, Atlacomulco

House in Cancún

Home of Ken Scott

Lighting the way up the many stairs in Ken Scott's house in Cuernavaca, these simple square glass fixtures keep the distinct mood of the house.

Opposite page: In no other place in the world is the flower pot a more loved household object than in Mexico; it is, in fact, the essence of the Mexican garden. Made of earthenware, sculpted from stone, lined with mirror fragments, in shapes and sizes too numerous to mention, flower pots adorn almost every Mexican house. Such is the Mexican's love of plants and flowers, that when they cannot afford flower pots, they will use anything at hand; old tin cans with their labels sometimes intact are filled with flowers and occupy every available space, so that no matter how poor the house is, it always looks colorful and gay.

Charmingly rounded, this carved stone urn glowing with red geraniums adds color to the entrance patio of the Rancho San Joaquin.

Home of Xavier Barbosa

Casa de las Campanas

This arrangement of flower pots of different sizes and shapes looks most attractive in an elegent colonial patio. These pots are made of unglazed earthenware and are planted with an assortment of small-leafed ivy, begonias, azaleas and geraniums. The large one in the foreground is amusingly decorated with a high relief showing a series of lizards chasing each other around it.

222

Tetelpa, Mexico City

Restaurant San Angel Inn

Although in different settings, these four flower pots have a certain likeness to each other. They are all made of unglazed earthenware and two of them show a woven basket pattern. The design of leaves and flowers decorating the lower one is now very rare.

The beautiful archeological piece (*below*) looks stunning in famous artist Rufino Tamayo's home and may have inspired craftsmen through the centuries.

Home of Alexander Kirkland

Home of Rufino and Olga Tamayo

Home of Federico Patiño

Wood also has its uses in this interesting field. Here are some ways in which wooden objects can be used to contain plants. Two antique corn grinders are made into planters for both indoor and outdoor use. They are preserved from humidity by coating the inside with a chemical substance that is not harmful to the plants. The bamboo and ferns look very much at home against the natural color of the wood. An old wooden cart, now filled with plants, makes an interesting feature in the hacienda of Atlacomulco.

Home of Xavier Barbosa

An ingenious idea for moving heavy
flower pots, these little wooden carts are
charming as well as practical.

Home of Jaume Ribas

Hacienda de Cortez, Atlacomulco

Restaurant San Angel Inn

Over this beautiful carved stone bench, a cut-out tin tree of life is planted with a pendulant sedum which is called *cola de borrego* (lamb's tail) in Mexico. At its side, growing from two big earthenware pots, are beautifully trained pyracanthus.

Home of Federico Patiño

226

Hacienda de Cortez, Atlacomulco

Home of Federico Patiño

This iron cart, once used in a silver mine, finds new life as an unusual plant container.

Flower pots are an integral component of these two wrought iron railings which are used as delicate space dividers in a Mexico City garden.

▽ *Home of Francisco and Amanda Martinez Negrete*   △ *Home of Dr. Mario Gonzalez Ulloa*   *Home of Elton and Martha Hyd*

Inspired by the ancient urns of classical design, these flower and plant filled versions lend dignity and grace to many patios and gardens. Of different shapes and materials, urns are the elegant cousins of the flower pot and, as such, are placed in the more visible and relevant parts of the house.

Home of Jack and Muriel Wolgin

Home of Elton and Martha Hyder

Home of Robert and Mary Buchner

229

Former Convento of Coixtlahuaca

Even in the most abandoned and foresaken buildings in Mexico, one finds that someone is interested enough to keep and care for a plant.

Opposite page: A striking ensemble is made by these different earthenware pots surrounding a stone Indian mission cross. The delicate plant with thorns and tiny red flowers called *corona de espinas* (crown of thorns) is aptly placed here.

Home of Robert Brady

Home of Robert Brady

Home of José and Dolores Yturbe

Home of Robert Brady

Used in the old sugar mills in the State of Morelos to store molasses, these thick, beautifully shaped pots are now considered collector's items.

Below: This photograph shows the striking contrast of these reddish brown water jugs against the stone wall.

Home of Edmundo O'Gorman

Casa Emília, Acapulco

In homes in Acapulco and other coastal areas, these flower pots planted with palms add a fresh green touch to shelters and outdoor living rooms.

House in Acapulco

House in Cancún

233

These two houses happily show the Mexicans' love for potted plants and flowers. Usually started from cuttings, rioting combinations of the more commonly found plants give their dwellings color and gaiety.

234

An old, cracked water storage tank makes a sunny perch for these containers filled with chrysanthemums and other floral odds and ends.

At the entrance to a little restaurant in Cuernavaca, these battered blue cooking pots are planted with fresh herbs for the kitchen.

Cuernavaca

The cactus in this little flower pot is the Echinocereus; its deep pink flowers are very large in relation to its size.

Echinocereus Cactus

Home of Karl Eric Noren

Nearly lost is the art of making these mirror-covered flower pots. In great demand in the nineteenth and early twentieth century, they were seen in corridors and arcades of the more affluent homes. There are still a few craftsmen who make them to order in the Crafts Market in downtown Mexico City. This well-preserved example brightens up the trellis balustrade in a San Miguel garden.

Home of Allen and Jeane-Claire Salsbury

A delightful assortment of differently shaped earthenware flower pots demonstrates the sense of humor which is the trade mark of the potters from the town of Acatlan in the State of Puebla. Animals are always favorite subjects; fish and frogs take their place at the edges of swimming pools and fountains.

me of Jack and Muriel Wolgin   *Villa Alejandra, Acapulco*

Above: The row of ceramic ducks makes a most charming and imaginative kitchen herb garden.

The coal-burning brazier becomes the base for an asparagus fern filled pot.

Home of Sloane Simpson

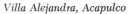

me of Ken Scott

Home of Allen and Jean-Claire Salsbury

An enchanting thought, this little basket, daily filled with fresh flowers, welcomes the visitor to Mr. and Mrs. Salsbury's home.

The kitchen patio is enlivened by these masonry planters filled with geraniums and dracaene and painted a deep terra cotta color to match the walls behind them.

Home of Milton and Sabina Leof

238

Home of Robert Brady

Home of Elton and Martha Hyder

At the entrance to one of San Miguel Allende's loveliest homes, the long balustrade carries these basket weave ceramic flower pots. Larger pots filled with bougainvillea in shades of purple, russet and deep red line this entranceway.

Set into these recessed arches, small flower pots add a delicate touch to a garden wall.

Tetelpa, Mexico City

240   The flower pot at its very best is depicted here. This finely modelled pair hold the round-shaped Indian laurel trees that frame this elegant doorway.

In Mexico, the garden does not only exist out of doors; it is often brought inside the house. Fruit and flowers are always arranged to their best advantage in markets and homes, and indoor plants give a touch of green to the interiors.

Set on a wide stone window ledge, this little fruit basket, skillfully arranged by famous painter Vicente Gandia, poetically displays the bounties of nature.

Home of Karl Eric Noren

242

With great imagination, Mr. Noren has converted a dark indoor area into this Moorish extravaganza. Mirrors line the walls, and white stucco arches reproduced from photographs of the Alhambra in Granada add to the illusion. In the center is a black marble fountain surrounded by potted palms and many colorful cushions and rugs.

Villa Alejandra, Acapulco

These large picture windows seem to bring the outdoors inside. The *piñanona* (split-leaf philodendron) spreads its fan-like leaves against the glass, forming a graceful pattern between the room and the view of the ocean.

Such is the sense of openness that this window creates, that
the old fig tree in the garden seems to be within arm's reach.

Home of Feliciano Bejar

One of the best places in the house in which to indulge in indoor gardening is the bathroom, since plants thrive in the steamy atmosphere.

The rough stone wall behind the window forms a screen as well as a small private garden for this tiled bathtub.

Ferns, impatiens and dumb cane in pots and planters bring an outdoor feeling into this elegant bathroom in Cuernavaca. Giving on to a sun terrace, this glassed-in bathroom becomes a practical greenhouse for the potted papyrus, philodendron and azalea in their large earthenware pots.

Home of Jack and Muriel Wolgin

Home of Oliver and Estelle Clapp

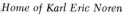

Home of Karl Eric Noren   *Home of Sloane Simpson*   *Home of Mario Gonzalez Ulloa, Jr.*

Behind the tiled tub, the owner has created a space for a planter. The carved stone shell takes the place of the usual tap. An attractive idea is the bouquet of fresh flowers placed in the little recess in the stone wall.

This plant holder of Oaxaca black clay makes an effective contrast against the white brick wall.

247

Home of Alexander Kirkland

An enchanting way to bring the outdoors inside is this little *nicho de concha* (shell niche) over a tiled fountain.

The carved and painted colonial angel entwined by maiden hair fern gives a lightness and simple grace to the otherwise extremely formal atmosphere of the living room.

Said to have come from an ancient Egyptian tomb, this wonderful, life-like tiger is also an original and comfortable seat.

Opposite page: A baroque wood angel seems to be holding up the entrance arch of a house in San Miguel de Allende. The maiden hair fern growing from the large ceramic urn gives it a lace-like background.

Home of Dr. Mario Gonzalez Ulloa

248

Home of Helen Ford

Two stately columns form an elegant division separating the outdoor planted area from the rest of the room. The section in the background is open to the sky, allowing the plants a total outdoor existence. In order to avoid flooding during heavy rains, light-colored gravel is loosely laid over the earth to allow good drainage. The whitewashed walls, uncarpeted dark floor and mellow antique furniture are truly complemented by the luxuriant greenery.

Home of Elton and Martha Hyder

Mrs. Hyder has both the most excellent taste and the best luck when it comes to finding extraordinary objects. This pair of rare terra cotta urns and bases frame an antique carved bench piled with orange and bright yellow cushions in the corridor of her San Miguel de Allende home.

El gusto por el color y el amor a las flores. - Pintó en San Angel. México D.F. Juan O'Gorman

Juan O'Gorman

Col. Bob and Nina Schalkwijk

This charming, fresh bouquet of yellow and deep pink roses by one of Mexico's best-known artists, Juan O'Gorman, is a departure from his usual style. His true vocation is mural painting, to which the walls of Chapultepec Castle in Mexico City bear glowing testimony.

253

The best known object in a garden in Mexico is the homemade twig broom, *escoba de jardin,* an absolute must without which the gardener feels totally despondent. No new-fangled or more serviceable substitute will ever take root in his heart.